HACKING

MADE EASY

Hack Your Way Through Life One Step at a Time

Dr. Robot

Computer Hacking

Table of Contents

An Introduction To Computer Hacking

Performing any modification of computer equipment and/or programming in order to achieve an action that was not the original intent of the inventor of either the machine or the programmed language is known as Computer Hacking. Those individuals who partake in such activities to achieve their desired effect within the described realm of computer hardware and software are popularly known as 'hackers', derived from the term 'hack' which has long been associated with a description of someone who is inept at his or her chosen profession, leading to the deduction that the hacker community as a whole is a bunch of rowdy youngsters who are wasting their time fixated on screens which is a wrong presumption of a highly specialized skill set that is the bane of modern multinational corporations and governments.

As a demographic population, Computer Hacking is an activity that is mostly common among the young, approximately the 15 to 35 age group who are members of generation 'X' and the millennial, predominantly male. This is not to say that the Computer Hacking is a casual hobby or an amateur pastime since there are countless hackers who can be deemed professionals and are renowned within the hacker community.

Delving into the subsets presents within such a diverse variety of hackers, the most prominent are by far the technology innovators who continuously strive to acquire new ways of meddling with computer functionality and treat their chosen field of interest as a higher calling requiring the utmost finesse and precision, the Pablo Picassos of the 21st century. As with any devoted professional, appreciation of the programming is at the core of their work, like medicine for doctors. Continuing with the analogy, hackers such as these become champion experts in a specific system pertaining to hacking, not because of the potential damage they can invariably cause if they so do desire but because it is an outlet of expression of their high order critical thinking abilities in order to demonstrate the heights of achieved potential acquired via perseverance, discipline and a love for what they do.

As described, it requires interest rather than a mandatory college curricula requirement to become proficient in the art of Computer Hacking, leading to large number of hackers who don't really possess diplomas or degrees, which makes their mastery of such a complex subject all the more amazing. A few farsighted companies having the vision have sought to employ such tech wiz magicians as part of their technical staff to search and report any defects in the security of their systems, finding flaws to be repaired urgently thus saving the company the acrimony of being infiltrated by an external source which are commonly corporate espionage missions, Inception in reality (pun intended). On a less sinister note, reward programs are also on offer such as by Facebook that pays $500 for every defect reported which is claimed via sleek black MasterCard.

Why do hackers hack?

Amongst the many reasons prescribed to the act of Computer Hacking, they all can be distilled down to 3 primary motives to hack either a stand-alone computer or an integrated network of such systems:

* The Individual Ego Boosting Justification. The hackers who ply their trade just for the fun of it. They target net connected computers, large servers, or main frame system frameworks for the privilege of demonstrating their superior prowess to their peers or to grasp and savor the progress they have made in advancing their skills to be able to take on more difficult challenges and test themselves to the fullest.

  The idea of breaching the safety of a computer for the beginner or novice, bypassing its firewall or other defenses, is no doubt very appealing as it grants you access to all the data present within it. The most lucrative aspect of all of this is the fact that the user is most of the time unaware that his or her computer has been searched for content and possibly been downloaded by someone else. Just imagine all the

Computer Hacking

music, photos, videos and all manner of private data at your disposal without anyone knowing. Does your arch nemesis have his awkward nude baby photos stored on his computer? Just hack into it and take those photos James Bond style and accidently 'leak' them on to social media. Enemy destroyed!

Thus, hacking is an amusing form of entertainment where you get to demonstrate your superior prowess in decimating all manner of protection in the form of firewalls and spywares.

- Monetary Benefits. As the famous saying goes, money makes the world go round. In the case of Computer Hacking, it remains by far the most attractive draw to even bother with learning the ins and outs of this rather mind boggling matter. But the rewards are great for those who hack as the targets are mostly the too big to fail banks and corporations sitting on an enormous pile of cash. The most recent example of such an endeavor was the attempt by a group of Bangladeshi hackers to steal one billion dollars of Bengali money kept with the Us Federal Reserve Bank. They succeeded, partially, as they managed to get 80 million dollars and would have easily walked away with the full Monty if it had not been for a typo mistake that set the alarms in action and alerted the management. Such an audacious attempt to get rich requires penetrating framework system computers that are to be found in such financial institutions. If you do not have the guts to tackle the big boys, such hacking attempts are also made on individual computers as people tend to foolishly store bank account information, social security number and credit card details which can be misused fairly easily.

A bit of advice to those tempted to perform such deeds. It's illegal. As much as one may want to flaunt the bad boy persona of a suave George Clooney in stealing another person's hard earned money, it would be better to tone down the boasting as you run the risk of getting caught and being send behind bars for your crime as even friends tend to tip off when envious by your ill-gotten gains.

If you want to play it safe, you cannot go wrong by adding connections to your site as it is a lot less conspicuous and allows you to get away with hacking without putting you in a fix. The way by which it works is that <u>web indexes see connections back to a site from different destinations of worth as a positive thing. These connections may help the site they connect to rank higher in the hunt postings.</u>

- The Archaist. The Tyler Durden of the hacking world. The Jokers who just want to see the world burn. Ultimate aim of a select few hackers, including hacker groups, is to cause the maximum amount of instability and disturbance as they possibly can. Be the thorn for as long and as much as possible. This is not to say that such objectives cannot have altruistic motives as the purpose can be to exhibit deficiencies in security protocol. But more often than not, the endgame is to literally destroy any organization for which there is hatred and contempt. The leaked I Cloud photos of celebrities known infamously as 'the fappening', the leaked email conversations of Sony, or the countless released account details of subscribers to Netflix etc. A lot of hacking gatherings have gained notoriety and become headline grabbing acts due to their antics such as LulzSec and Anonymous (the Guy Hawkes mask man you see on CNN).

To sail alone or with a crew is a personal decision but once you are in the gang, there usually is no going back unless you are comfortable living in Stone Age without electricity. You have been warned.

Having read the above mentioned reasons for hacking, one may assume that all that Hackers do is cause as much mayhem as possible. This is not always the case as Hackers also break into frameworks and fix any lapse in security openings which are neglected by the owners and are left in disarray and serve as soft targets for the less well intentioned. Moreover, it is brought to the client's attention of such security openings which they themselves cannot fix. Lastly, any frameworks destroyed by bad hackers are repaired by the good hackers in order to keep the universe in balance.

Such instances of Samaritans are rare at best since the bad guys outnumber the good guys by a fair margin. So do act in surprise like you would if a superhero suddenly appeared but also be wary that it won't happen every time when you are in trouble.

Chapter 1: Essential Hacking Tools and Skills

SQLI Helper

For defenseless websites that are using SQL infusion and are to be hacked, then the first choice remains the SQLI Helper as it saves plenty of time since futile attempts are not wasted in trying out different mixes and codes in order to gain access to the website. Moreover, the need to learn SQL is avoided with the use of SQL Helper as it is very effective and simple at what it does. All you really have to do is to direct the SQL Helper on what to do and where exactly to look.

Dark Port Scanner

Dark Port Scanner is employed in order to carefully look for any open ports on a network which is to be hacked.

Sonic Bat - The Batch File Virus Creator

As the name suggests, this particular system makes clump infections that are referred to as a 'batch' which are in the format of (.bat) and so the name of   Sonic Bat-Batch File Virus Creator which has dramatically shifted the paradigm in how to destroy the computer to be targeted and is therefore offering more choice and a different method to achieve this aim.

The prime mode of action is to unleash a surge onto the ROM or storage capacity in layman terms by creating a large number of documents in different files, kind of like jamming paper to the brim into file cabinets, and thus rendering the capacity to full causing to fully utilize the computer's 'envelope surge'. A side effect or ancillary action in this operation is to incorporate the (.bat) extension to exe convertor and thereby converting the whole of infection records into exe infection programs along with a symbol changer.

Brutus (Password Cracker)

As the subtitle clearly makes it obvious, Brutus happens to be a password cracker that acts remotely to carry out its objective when the websites or programming protocols in question are HTTP, POP3, FTP, SMB, Telnet, Parcels and others. Points to note with regard to use of Brutus is that it runs mainly on Windows Operating Systems meaning any computer having Windows 2000, 9x, NT and above. The exception to all of this is that there is no variant available or accessible for UNIX Operating System which is a letdown if you are amongst those users but the outlook remains bright since it will probably come out sooner rather than later . The icing on the cake is that the program is free for anyone to download and use.

As per the history of this illustrious software, Brutus was developed in the spring of 1998 and made available for public download the same year and at the last count has been downloaded at least 70,000 times and an approximate number of 200,000 people have visited the developer's page. By way of donations, the program has undergone graduated improvements that have prompted new release versions many of which have been utilized and the remaining updates are made available as the case maybe. From humble beginnings where Brutus was used mainly in checking for changes in default and regular passwords that were in vogue once upon a time to the high tech code breaking for which Brutus is used for today..

IP Tools

IP-Tools are the all in one comprehensive system by which users can access TCP/IP utilities. And like the above-mentioned Brutus program happens to be free of cost to the end user as a freemium hacking program. IP-Tools are compatible for a lot of Operating Systems such as Linux, Macintosh, and the whole range of Windows Operating Systems from Windows 95 onwards that includes Windows 98, Windows ME, Windows NT 4.0, Windows 2000, Windows XP, Windows 2003, Windows XP SP 1 to 3 Windows Vista, Windows 7, Windows 8/8.1 and the recently released Windows 10.

As per its capabilities, it is a vital component for anyone who so wishes to use the Internet or a more localized setup in the form of an Intranet within a college or company. IP-Tools have the below mentioned 'tools' that are commonly utilized:

1. Local Info – Gives a brief overview of the underlying system specification that serve as the neighborhood host of the attached or connected computers in the setup. As such, it gives information about the processor (speed, core, manufacturer), memory (RAM in terms of GB and ROM in terms of GB and TB), Winsock information, and so on.

2. Name Scanner – Looks at all the domain names or host names as present within the domain of IP locations which is represented in the form of numerical digits separated by decimals and serve as identification tags.

Computer Hacking

3. Port Scanner – Similar to port scanner but instead of IP locations which are static in nature, it scans the network or multiple networks for dynamic TCP based administrations.

4. Ping Scanner – Not to be confused with table tennis, a ping scanner serves to ping a remote over the system regardless of the physical distance.

Cain and Abel

Now for a departure from scheduled programming to discuss sibling rivalry on a biblical scale. Just kidding! The program Cain and Abel (also shortened to just "Cain" in hacking parlance) is a Windows based password recovery program. Simply put, it is the locksmith you go to when you lose the key to your computer treasure. It is a comprehensive program in its said category and differs from the preceding description of hacking tools used for soliciting illegal access as it the 911 helpline when a passcode has been forgotten or lost by the original user in most of the cases. Cain and Abel utilize various techniques to recover every conceivable sort of passwords under the sun.

The Essential Skills to Becoming a Master Hacker

Like any professional calling, it takes time, discipline, commitment and dedication to be truly proficient at what you do. Becoming a hacker is no different and is unique in the sense that elements of both data analytics and creativity are required which makes it distinct among the computer science disciplines. Any hacker worth its salt has to be abreast with all the current Information Technology advancements and up to date with recent procedures and methodology employed. To make it even more difficult, this criteria gets even tougher when it comes to being a Jedi Master of hacking as it demands Yoda-like command over numerous abilities. I have listed the salient abilities down below and try not to think of it as an obstacle but a challenge for you to overcome and dominate. As you go through the list, you will find that some skills require more time to acquire than others which should be taken in your stride. Do not be dejected as a journey of a thousand mile begins with a single step as over time you will definitely have a decent level of expertise just by being patient with yourself. Without further ado, this is checklist you have to tick off and master, pardon my Star Wars references, to become the Han Solo of Computer Hacking.

A. The Fundamental Skills

1. Basic Computer Skills

To point out the obvious, hacking requires you to be able to effectively use a computer, whether it is a desktop or laptop. This goes beyond simply turning on the system and thinking that AOL is the internet, which was acceptable for grandparents in the 90s. One therefore has to be computer literate and simply knowing how to type a few words on Microsoft Word or spending countless hours on Facebook does not count. As an example, you can consider yourself above this grade if you have the capability to use the order line in the Windows Operating System, change the registry settings, and set up parameters for your independent system administration.

2. Organizing Skills

Continuing with the theme of system administration, it is necessary to be able to comprehend the fundamentals of systems administration before grasping the intricacies inherent in its management, such as:

- DHCP

- NAT

- Subletting

- IPv4

- IPv6

- Public v Private IP

- DNS

- Routers and switches

- VLANs

- OSI model

- MAC tending to

- ARP

This may seem like an overly exhaustive list that may seem fruitless in trying to become a computer hacker. But ignore them at your own peril as even though advances are made on an almost daily frequency in this vastly interesting field, the better you know the functionality of the basics, the more

Computer Hacking

successful you will be. Mentioned below are additional sources that may be of help to the interested reader in order to broaden their horizon. There is no conflict of interest as they were not written by the author but have been referenced as they are exceptionally useful in offering clear cut instructions alongside covering a sizeable portion of basic system administration as described before:

• Hacker Fundamentals: A Tale of Two Standards

• The Everyman's Guide to How Network Packets Are Routed

3. Linux Skills

While a few programs were mentioned previously that were primarily Windows based, it goes without saying that a hacker needs to have or acquire high levels of Linux familiarity to be any good because the tools for the trade are produced for Linux. The main reason is that Linux allows more room and space to carry out hacking tasks that are intrinsically not possible when using any version of a Windows Operating System.

As with organizing skills, the reader is referenced to go through the below mentioned text that was authored by yours truly as it is probably the only guide you need to get into the Linux Operating System for purposes of Hacking.

- Linux Basics for the Aspiring Hacker

4. Virtualization

You would not expect to ace your exams without going through a few practice tests. Ditto is the case with hacking where you try out your 'hacks' in virtualization programming bundles such as the aptly named Virtual Box or the equally good VMware Workstation. Never be too confident or arrogant that your hacks are going to be fool proof without going through a trial run and these program offer the opportunity to go for a trial run before hitting the big time in the real world (pun intended).

5. Security Concepts & Technologies

As the saying goes, offense is the best form of defense and any hacker worth its salt would be wise to add a working knowledge of all the recent security advances made in bolstering up the system against hacker penetration and it's your job to know such safeguards in order to always be a step ahead. In that, hacking is a cat and mouse game where you have to assume the role of Jerry in always outsmarting Tom. The only way is by being aware of the tricks employed by security administrators and this task is made digestible

Computer Hacking

by beginning with getting acquainted with terms such as PKI (open key infrastructure), SSL (secure attachments layer), IDS (interruption discovery framework), firewalls, and how they apply to hacking. A great starting point in boosting up your abilities is to complete a base level security course such as Security+ and going through different texts available on the subject such as

- How to Read & Write Snort Rules to Evade an IDS

B) The Intermediate Skills

Having gone through the teething stage of computer hacking, next up is the awkward teen years where you get to experiment with which aspect of hacking intrigues you the most and likewise can be bit of a roller-coaster ride in terms of cementing your skills in face of increasing difficulty while still managing to maintain your interest. Getting a good grip on the upcoming described skills will enable you to get a clearer picture and plan when trying to pull of your future hacks.

6. Web Applications

Boys are separated from men in this key area. Majority of the hackers call themselves so solely based on their mastery of Web applications which just shows how important this is to truly become a hacker. This is a gradual process where you get better each time you invest your time and energy in seeing how the databases and web applications interact with each other in making the Internet work as it does with your returns being manifold to make you more proficient. This is an essential skill to master as almost every hacker assembles their own web page to carry out the time engraved activity of phishing and other like activities to deceive. The reader is directed to search for the following texts to broaden their horizons and be the best of what they can be by mastering a few basic maneuvers employed in web applications for hacking purposes:

- How to Clone Any Website Using Track

- How to Redirect Traffic to a Fake Website

- The Ultimate List of Hacking Scripts for Metasploit's Meterpreter

7. Database Skills

A topic that is related to web applications but is well beyond that scope in broadening your arsenal for launching effective hacks is the area of network databases. Not only a theoretical knowledge of how databases function but also a comprehensive understanding of the inherent defects that can be exploited for your gain. A roadmap to get you on your way would be to first get fully acquainted with the SQL dialect and then gradually proceed to master of the big DBMS's like Oracle, Myself and SQL Server. As always, the desire to learn must come from within which involves searching for authoritative books on the field and the below mentioned seminal texts are a good starting point:

- The Terms & Technologies You Need to Know Before Getting Started

- Hunting for Microsoft's SQL Server

- Cracking SQL Server Passwords & Owning the Server

- Hacking Myself Online Databases with Slap

- Separating Data from Online Databases Using Slap

8. Advanced TCP/IP

From the beginning, you must pay attention to be able to understand and conceptualize TCP/IP basics. Only then will you have certifiably be an intermediate hacker as the ability to manipulate TCP/IP convention stack and fields and the associated subtlety in doing so in a conspicuous manner. One of the main things that are covered under this topic is to incorporate fields such as banners and windows in both

TCP and IP, along with doing so against the casualty framework to allow for Mitt assaults.

9. Cryptography

Not a skill which you have to master but a working knowledge is necessary in order to go about your task as greater understanding of calculative cryptography will give you more leverage in dominating this aspect. If for nothing else, knowing cryptography will allow the hacker to ensure secrecy of their hacking activities and thus enable him to avoid getting caught.

C) The Intangible Skills

The difference between a chef and cook is the fact that a cook knows how things are done whereas a chef knows why it is done. To be the hacker that everyone looks up to as an example to emulate one must acquire a 'feel 'of hacking such that you have a finger on the next big thing, an intuitive feel of doing things that others cannot dream of, being where the puck is going rather than where it has gone. A salient overview of such abilities is:

10. Persistence

If at first you don't succeed, hack and hack again. Hacking comes under those things that are learned over a long period of time, not considering the lifelong commitment to keep up with all the developments that spring up every week in this ever expanding universe. So if you are in it for the laughs than I am sorry to disappoint as even learning to hack your crush's Facebook account is a gigantean task. Therefore do keep at it as improvement will come gradually and it will be months after you can show something for all your hard work. It is only be being constantly motivated will you be able to reach a level of hacking secured frameworks for money or fun. Believe me; the journey is worth the destination you will surely reach.

11. Think Creatively

Hacking is like a game of chess sometimes. There is no one solid way to go about as there are many variations in getting setup to attempt a hack. More often than not, you will come up against security defenses such as firewalls will require you to think on your heels and think of a roundabout way to get the hack done, often thinking so within a minute's notice. A good guide will be to look at the below text for inspiration:

- Null Byte's Guide to Social Engineering

- Crypto Locker: An Innovative & Creative Hack

12. Problem-Solving Skills

Remember those algebra assignments that had you tearing your hair out at the sheer pointlessness of the whole shebang. That indeed had a purpose, apart from getting you admitted to a psych ward. Though you may have crystal clear concepts but the ability to apply those ideas to seemingly novel situations is the one that matters. So make it a habit to think logically rather than going through a rote learned routine. A simple advice is to breakdown the problem into small pieces and get about solving them in sequential steps to get to a solution. As with every challenge, practice is the only policy without which you cannot hope to program in hacking. The same is true for life in general.

Chapter 2: What is Malware and the basics

Malware stands for malicious software which is really any program or software intended to cause disturbance in normal computer functioning, create abnormal data files or simply to allow the developer to obtain access to the computer which has inadvertently installed malware unintentionally. What sets the nature of Malware apart from other ingenious harm causing techniques is the unexpected violent behavior of the program which acts to render the use of computer null and void. Malware is developed with the explicit intent to cause damage and comes under the encompassing term of Barware which also includes programming that is having flaws in its code and therefore causes harm that was not the original purpose and can be likened to a bug.

Other source of confusion as far as semantics are concerned is the term 'Aware' which can be used for stealth surveillance as in keeping a tab on the target's computer for a predetermined period of time or for retrieving data stored on the computer in a manner that deflects attention from the user. An example would be the program Reign for the above mentioned purposes. Aware can also be used for causing a nuisance to the end user in either causing trouble in normal functioning or locking up the computer so that no one can use it at all. An example would be the blackmail program 'Crypto Locker' in which the user has to pay a certain amount of money, via credit card or bit coins. This has the added disadvantage of giving away your credit card information as well. In sharp contrast, the term Malware is distinguished from Aware in that Malware is a wider term that pertains to a mostly damaging program or software of which notable examples include terms such as spyware, worms, computer infections, Trojan software, ransom ware, scare ware etc. Malware can therefore take up multiple forms with a singular motive having different types of underwritten code and scripts. In order to get access or be installed on the computer, Malware comes in a hidden form dressed up as a benign update to regular pre-installed programs or hidden within innocuous documents or email attachments. As the software that comes under Malware is so vast, trends regularly arise in what gets to be more widely used. As of 2016, the trend of using viruses and worms is on the decline with Trojans being the more popular option as anti-virus software still has a hard time figuring out this threat and therefore is in vogue amongst hackers who want to cause trouble. Though Malware has been around for many years, by some accounts from the advent of the Internet, the laws concerning its restriction and punishment are woefully limited, much to the delight of many hackers.

But be warned, a few countries and states in the U.S have strict punishment if caught distributing Malware.

Trojans

The name is taken from Greek Mythology and is a good description of this popular program in which a malicious program or software having a harmful code encrypted within it is lodged inside an apparently safe file, document, software or program. When present within a computer, the Trojan software takes control of the functioning capability of the said system causing one of many things. The Trojan can cause to change all the passwords, change the file directory, and place all the installed authentic software under lock down. If an extreme Trojan has infected your system, then the possibilities are direr as your entire memory stored on your hard drive can be wiped out or the processor made to work so fast that it heats up and burns. In the modern age, Trojans have been reported that have automatically used the auto upload function available on many photo editors such as Picasa to post images online on your social media account like Facebook, Instagram, Twitter.

Viruses

The computer virus is amongst the most well-known malware becoming part of the common slang. As such people tend to label all such malware that may have infected their computer as a virus which may not be always the case. The virus is indeed the most common malware to affect any individual computer or a computer network. Such is its presence that all computer protective software is termed as anti-virus. So what is a virus? A virus is any line of code which has been installed on the system or framework without the consent of the user and has the purpose of causing the malfunctioning of the system. The virus, like its biological counterpart, has the ability to replicate itself and transfer itself via the intranet, the Internet, or simply via USB. What distinguishes a virus from any nonsense code is the fact that a virus was made by a human with the intent of causing harm rather than not functioning at all. Without such a versatility in its destructive ability, it may seem amazing to know that a virus is really simple to create but do not be fooled by its simplicity: Virus can be extremely lethal since they tend to take up all the available ROM and put the network or the computer to a stop as far as operation is concerned. There are different types of viruses but can be broadly divided into simple and complex viruses as for hacking purposes. Simple viruses tend to affect only one computer and are not having the ability to replicate.

These are easily spotted by anti-virus program and the best suite for this purpose is by Norton. The other type of virus, Complex viruses, are having the ability to replicate and can transfer from one computer to another over various networks.

Worms

A rather tame version or type of malware is known as the worm. Worms are a kind of malware that can be seen as discrete or independent in that they do not have to attach themselves to a preexisting program, software or data file/document and has the ability to replicate it. Therefore, the difference between a worm and a virus is that worm can exist as a separate program whereas virus has to be attached to something. The similarity of course is that both can replicate themselves under certain circumstances. But specifically for worms, their main and sole function is to spread to other computers and make duplicate copies for itself in order to consume as much memory (ROM) as possible. Worms are not as dangerous as many of the other malware mentioned in this book and tend only to take up space and will not cause any damage to your computer or its functioning. Only by scanning the computer using detection software will the worms be detected and removed. Like viruses, worms are relatively simple to create and distribute. They are no longer used much by hackers looking to create mischief and are not much of a concern in terms of worrying about the possible repercussions.

Spyware

Spyware is that category of Malware where the damage or harm caused to the computer itself is minimal or nonexistent. The real purpose of spyware, as the name aptly suggests, is to screen the computer of user for any valuable information which is stored via an in built algorithm and is subsequently transmitted whenever the system us connected to the computer. It does this by sending batch files to the computer whose IP address is stored within the spyware to which the batch file is sent. If on the other hand a computer is continuously connected to the Internet then a live stream of sorts is continuously transmitted to the user whose IP address is the receiver in the spyware code. Thus there are two types of spyware and now days both types are assimilated into a single program. Spyware is distributed secretly as part of freemium software that is available for download or downloads itself without the user having to get a covering program by having the user click on a download button which directs him to another site but which in reality actually leads to the transfer and installation of spyware on the computer. The main target of spyware, once it gets installed in the computer, is to take screenshots at a regular interval or cache the typing that the user does and store it in a .txt file. Then the images and text file are transferred having the data. This can then be sieved through for information pertaining to Credit Card Information, Social Media account passwords etc.

Bots

You may have experienced having to write a 'captcha' image in order to make an account for email, social media accounts or just simply in registering for a poll or commenting on news websites. If you pay attention, it is mentioned quite often that this is done so to prove that you are not a 'Bot'. The end game is to have made so many accounts that can be used for clicking ads to earn money or spamming a comments thread. Therefore a bot is any computer in which a malware program has installed that keeps on doing a monotonous task over and over again either on the Internet, as described clearly in the above mentioned examples, or on a stand-alone computer to produce meaningless documents or folders to take up space.

They are a few terms with which a person can get confused with when learning about bots. The term 'boot' is used for the bunch of client framework system that is hooked onto being part of the overall scheme to get multiple computers to perform as a bot. Each bot is an equal part of a boot, sorry for the similar semantics, and also communicate with each other without interference of the original creator. For the end purpose, each bot is independent along with being a master over the partner bots. There does come a point when the user of the computer alters the activities of his computer that has been turned into a bot. This alteration is known as the client's privilege which occurs when the bot has done his bit before being over ridden by the client, known as the client's right to change his own configuration, colloquially known as 'banners' and such bots become redundant and become 'hailed bots'.

Ransom ware

As the name puts it Ransom ware is a sort of malware that acts like a lunch room bully where it demands a payment to be made in order to access different components of the computer such as accessing the web browser, opening word documents, or opening images and playing videos. This was an example of an individual computer. On the scale of framework, ransom ware acts to prevent access of the end users to the mainframe computer or server and the access is granted by paying a small amount which is transferred to the creator of the ransom ware either through a credit card transfer or bit coin. As with any other malware program, there are many variations as to how it goes about its action. A ransom ware program known as Crypto Locker causes to encode records and renders them useless to the user who cannot access the records unless a payment is made. For the transfer of money, the dark internet is used for which a different internet explorer called 'torr' is used in order to hide C&C interchanged.

Ransom ware is also known as a shareware of sorts as it enables 'sharing' (even though its coerced) of one person's money to another as it cloaks the transfer of currency under a legal cover so as to not be detected by a policing authority. With that legal cover, the shareware or ransom ware in effect terrifies or scares the user to pay a nominal amount in order to operate the computer. Therefore ransom ware emulates FAKEAV malware in its end goal but uses a different methodology. For sake of clarity, FAKEAV malware wants the user to purchase software or program instead of a direct transfer of money.

Root kit

Root kit is a set of applications or utilities that is employed for every other malware program in order to hide the identity of these programs from being detected. The way by which Root kit works is that small parts of the operating framework like unused RAM, redirecting capability, and Operating System programming to make the malware hidden to being detected by Anti-Virus software.

If you are the hacker interested in distributing malware, it is important to procure the right root kits as they can be the real deal or just fluff. To ensure your malware scams do not get caught it is vital that you make sure that the root kit is genuine. So it is imperative upon you to run anti root kit software to make sure that your root kit is up to the task.

Adware

Adware is the name given to the deceptive program which is on its own legitimate and works fine at its assigned task but has accessory advertisements attached with it in lieu of free use of the program. You all may have encountered this sort of software in the form of free games that make you see all the ads and give you the option to remove them by paying $0.99(as is usually the case). Free games are simply a drop in the ocean as far as adware is concerned as they also include photo editing software, Emulators, club apps etc. The adware method is a great way to boost the popularity of the developer or programmer as people are more likely to download the free product and if they like using it then, more often than not, they will gladly pay for the convenience of having an ad free experience. In a way, it is a gradual progression from ads that used to appear on the web browsers which met their demise with ad blockers to adware. If and when you purchase the right to use the premium app, then the ads should stop appearing. Be sure to make that happen when you design your adware software.

Chapter 3: Using Software for Hacking

Now to the meat of the whole shebang, the main course of the meal. Having mastered so many different skills pertaining to the use of computer and learning the basics of how hacking is used in the form of different applications, we get to the part of using the software specifically geared towards hacking. A wide range of programs and suites are at your disposal to do your bidding. This chapter will sort the gold from the garbage as only a few hacking software are up to the mark and worth your time. As you read through the chapter, you will encounter my specially curated list of programs designed to hack passwords and systems along with engaging in sniffing about for vital data that is of your interest and is targeted by you to be retrieved. At the same time, I don't want your understanding of hacking to be simply restricted to the use of hacking software. Actually, hacking software is used for social gathering of data for mild level hacking that is also colloquially known as a passive form of data gathering.

1. Nap -The Network Mapped:

First up is the one of the most over used system mapping utility program that is primarily employed for the examination and recognition of network ports and

Operating System Frameworks along with the overview of administration and functioning of the described system. As for the Operating systems that have the ability to run Nap include both Windows (all versions from 95 to 8.1) and Linux. It is pertinent to mention that Linux is more compatible for using Nap and is therefore recommended to use if hacking is the main purpose.

2. John the Ripper Password Cracker

As the name aptly suggests, this software program is utilized as a password cracker, or more accurately, password wafer and is the most effective at what it does. It is used primarily when the password to be hacked is present on the Operating System such as UNIX, DOS, Win32, OpenVMS etc. But the prime function of this program is to hack passwords stored on the UNIX Operating System. At the same time, John the Ripper (JTR) can be used to separate the weak passwords from the strong passwords.

3. Nesses Remote Security Scanner

When cheapskate organizations do not want to hire hackers to do security reviews, they rely on this software suite to scan for loopholes in the firewall set up to protect the system framework from invasion. Nesses used to be open source in the not so distant past but now have turned to a shut source for the lack of regular updates in the programming code. It has remained a free software and for the amateur freelance hacker and a company that does not have a large budget to protect its IT department, Nesses makes for a great alternative for a quick, cheap security review.

4. Wire shark – The Sniffer

This software was also called by the name Ethereal. In effect it acts as an investigative program which truly acts like a sniffer to sniff out and scan any systemic edges present within the system framework. This analyzer is available in the form of an open source software that can be edited anyone. Wire shark is the premium sniffer available on the market and is the preferred choice of hackers worldwide. Two main reasons for its enduring popularity are that it has an interactive graphical user interface and can be run on both Windows and Linux Operating System.

5. Eraser

Even when we delete things from the recycle bin, a cache of our data remains on the hard drive and cannot be completely removed until it gets gradually full with other data. This is an important point to note as neither multiple formatting or resetting the Operating System to its original setting will do the trick. The actual recommended method by the U.S F.B.I is to corrupt the hard Drive by taking it out of its case and running a magnet over it to be 100% sure. Falling short of this, the next best thing is to get the software known as Eraser. This program is available for only Windows OS and is compatible with many of its versions from 95 onwards. Eraser does the task by overwriting the hard drive multiple times with an algorithm to incorporate useless lines of code while at the same time keeping it formatted for further use. As with other hacking software, Eraser is also open source for updates that mimic real life conditions and continues to be free to this very day.

6. LCP – Windows Password Cracker

Up till now we have mentioned a few top quality password breakers and among the very best is the LCP program which is available for free and is only compatible with the different versions of the Windows Operating System. Its counterpart for Linux is not yet available at the time of writing this e-book. As with other password breakers, LCP also utilizes different methods in order to get the job done. The prominent modes include brute force, word reference assault & half and half assault. With such a wide arsenal of attacks, it comes as no surprise that LCP is the go to option when we need to import account related data., have our passwords recuperated, or for figuring out hashes.

7. Cain & Able Passwords Cracker

The program Cain and Abel (also shortened to just "Cain" in hacking parlance) is a Windows based password recovery program. Simply put, it is the locksmith you go to when you lose the key to your computer treasure. It is a comprehensive program in its said category and differs from the preceding description of hacking tools used for soliciting illegal access as it the 911 helpline when a passcode has been forgotten or lost by the original user in most of the cases. Cain and Abel utilize various techniques to recover every conceivable sort of passwords under the sun

8. SuperScan- Port Scanner

Another must have program is the SuperScan, shortened to Supers, which is another of the TCP/IP port scanner that can recognize open ports within the set IP ranges. As for specifications, SuperScan has a graphical user interface and is compatible with different versions of Windows OS. Being so simple to use, it should also be your first choice.

9. Nekton – CGI Scanner

Continuing with the topic of scanners, we will touch upon the topic of a great CGI scanner, Nekton, that is Open Source like many of the programs mentioned and is directed against web servers for almost everything imaginable. It has a quick and fast action to analyze multiple servers to a number ranging from 2500 to 6000.

10. Pouf

Pouf is used for the identification of the working framework on servers such as SYN Mode, SYN+ACK mode, RST+ mode, or any machines whose interchanges you wish to monitor for activity. The underlined code that makes Pouf function is a passive apparatus that uses fingerprinting for analysis and identification.

Email Hacking

One of the commonest form of hacking there is , Email hacking is the illegal access to the email account of an individual or corporation for viewing the email chats and all the record of emails stored on the server. As you may read regarding the Hillary Clinton email scandal, she employed her own web server instead of the designated official one. Email hacking in essence involves hacking into the web server that acts as host to the email storage and transfer. The most common approach employed by hackers to get into the server's pants is called a phishing assault, a term that you have encountered so many times before already, especially when related to the hackers from the developing countries. The people who fall for it are many as it targets the social media users who cannot distinguish a secured web portal from a fake generated one. There are two sorts of phishing assault: Normal Phishing and Desktop Phishing.

The premise behind phishing is fairly simple. A redirection is made to a site that is constructed to be as real to the actual one. For example, you get on your friend's Wi-Fi and try to log in on Facebook. You will not notice that the web page is not actually from Facebook but a fake one hosted by your friend. After you have logged in your details, a copy of your input will be made and stored and you directed to the original website. Now your supposed friend will use this data and can do anything with it while you will be stunned as to how it could have happened to you.

Once the basic concept behind phishing is clear, the following steps are in order to get started on your own to take revenge:

1. First, make your own website that can be easily done using Dreamweaver and hosted on a free web hosting website.

2. Then you have to follow this up by shifting the phished onto the document index of the website.

3. Alongside, you will have to deal with another document named "login.php" that will allow you to store the username and password input by your intended victim.

4. Alter the phished so that the username and password input is also spared for use onto the original site.

5. Enjoy the fruits of your labor as the hacking part begins!

The Directory consists of:-

I. index.html

ii. Index files

iii. Login.php

iv. Login.txt

6. You will have to subtly direct the intended victim to use your phished website by either suggestion or a casual remark that will trigger his use of that website, like saying what the price of a soccer ball is and he will open Amazon.

7. You can access all the data input by accessing your web hosting record of administration and open the login.txt to view email id and password.

8. Done.

Operating system Hacking

Hacking requires time and commitment to master and demands discipline and patience as you work towards achieving your goal. One of the main things that torment would be hackers is the legality of it all. For those interested, there is a whole discussion on ethical hacking in chats, reddits and discussion boards all over the Internet. My personal opinion is that hacking cannot be stopped so why bother putting up so many useless restrictions rather it is more beneficial to ingrain the limits of what we can do so that the privacy of individuals and security of companies is protected within a reasonable limit. As you continue on this journey, you will come across many such dilemmas. One source of contention is the Operating System used by hackers and the Operating Systems that are most vulnerable to hacking. Below is a discussion on all such matters.

1. Kali Linux :-

If there ever was a must have software, then it is definitely Kali Linux for the hacker who wants to take his game to the next level. It uses a propelled entrance testing device. This technique uses a variety of measures to test the weakness present within the current security arrangement. Kali is the only thing you need if your aim is to test the limits of the incorporated OS. It utilizes 300 different apparatuses, all of them being open source.

2. Backtrack 5r3

After years of improvement, Backtrack has earned a reputation of a comprehensive security review software suite that is utilized by hackers to detect flaws in any arrangement they wish to hack. Such is its popularity that Backtrack is employed by security experts in computer defense all over the world.

3. Back Box Linux:-

Similar to Backtrack, Back Box is geared towards performing infiltration tests and security assessments. Back Box is based on a Linux conveyance that copies the underling code of a previous iteration, the Bunt program. With a graphical user interface, Back Box is easy to use, is incredibly fast and slick at what it does, and with the added benefit of it is being continually updated so that the hacking maneuvers carried out remain effective against the most recent security upgrades.

4. Samurai Web Testing Framework

The Samurai Web Testing Framework is a web pen-testing environment that uses the live Linux background which has been configured to its limit. It contains the best of both the open source code that is appreciated by hackers to meddle around with and free apparatuses which allow for extensive testing and assaulting on sites whether they are vulnerable or not.

5. Node Zero Linux:-

Authority tools are needed for testing the ease of hacker access to a system framework and examination of the security arrangements. It has a characteristically unique way of bringing about its task since it brings all the information in an easily digestible form.

The Node Zero Linux is best used for a batch testing of the program under question as it is best when large amounts of data is to be gathered for analysis but can also be employed for live feed of any immediately occurring security flaws. It is primarily run on the Linux Operating System.

6. Kopi STD:-

Security software that runs only on Linux Operating System, Kopi STD (Sexually Transmitted Disease) is a collection of multiple security instruments that are available to have their underlying code changed by anyone that is they are open source. The purpose of this software is to aggregate all the security devices to make them available at your disposal to cause harm and damage.

7. **Canine:-**

Canine stands for computer aided investigative environment which is a venture of digital forensics made in collaboration with an Italian gnu/Linux live conveyance.

It is a complete measurable environment made up of programming devices that coordinate to form programming modules and give an interactive graphical interface that makes the user experience more friendly and easy to use.

WPA2 Hacking

Wi-Fi Protected Access (WPA) and Wi-Fi Protected Access II (WPA2) are two of the most used terms associated with security when it comes to wireless internet connections, or Wi-Fi. Just because they are supposedly securing the wireless doesn't mean they cannot be hacked as was the case with the previous security benchmark of Wired Equivalent Privacy or WEP.

Requirements:

1. Remote card which is supporting the unique wanton mode.

2. Access point with WPA2 and WPS empowerment.

Wi-Fi Hacking to gain access to WPA2 connection:

1. Open the terminal (CTRL+ALT+T) and sort airmon-ng.

2. Stop the remote screen mode by running airmon-ng stop wlan0

3. By running airodump-ng wlan0 our remote interface will begin catching the information.

4. Discovery of access point with encryption.

Calculate WPA2 and note the AP channel number. Our concern is whether the target AP has WPS empowered. If the case is that the WPS Locked statuses is No, then proceed to step 5.

5. Split the WPA2 password utilizing reader.

Reader -I <your interface> -b <Wi-Fi casualty MAC address> –fail-wait=360

Data procured from step 3 will be:

Reader -I wlan0 -b E0:05:C5:5A:26:94 –fail-wait=360

Time taken to split the password depends on the computer's processing power.

Chapter 4: Hackers arsenal: Common Techniques and Viruses

Common Techniques and Viruses

The preparation and planning involved in successfully executing a hacking is no mean feat or at the very least something that requires a lot of grey matter. If you think that hacking was just going to be about installing and running a program with you sitting back and chilling, then I am sorry to burst your bubble as the complexities involved and the variables under consideration are enough to make anyone's head spin. What is more often the norm is the use of different strategies in the face of presenting outcomes which are prepared beforehand to make best use of the time as the window in which a hacker can make his assault successful is very narrow. It is only by expecting the worst and having a mix of high artillery and soft techniques can you hope to penetrate defenses more times than not. Viruses come under those soft techniques that are routinely employed by the hackers to eat up the defenses from inside so that the firewall of the system framework network can be more easily breached by the hacker in question.

Social Engineering:

Social engineering has different facets to offer in terms of hacking potential and a wide spectrum of individuals utilize the deceptiveness inherent in the fabric of social engineering , both for illegal purposes and by professional hackers. It is not technical wizardry or difficult to do, but is in fact your personal relationship skills at the human level. Never forget that the Midas touch in hacking is how effectively you can read the mind of your intended victim. Use of realistic graphic illustrations, understanding and comforting tone in your content, having an air of reliability oozing from each and every action that you take makes all the difference between a successful hacker and one that will only wonder why he could not make it to the big league

The Virtual Probe:

One vivid example to demonstrate the power of social building as it pertains to computer hacking is seen in the use of the virtual probe, used officially by merchants in data recollection. A counter intuitive offer is made like on those annoying TV ads that offer a surprisingly good offer, the one you really cannot resist. You will also employ that very same tactic in offering a return on investment that is too good to be true, which is what it turns out to be. Excited and not wanting to miss out on the amazing opportunity, the victim will willingly hand over sensitive private information such as bio data, credit card information which the opportunistic hacker will use to his utmost benefit.

Lost Password:

You can go through the most well thought off master plan to take down your target but the most effective method remains the one which is the simplest. The smart hacker will acquire the client data pertaining to his account name and password. Now no one is stupid enough to give the information straight out but they will happily hand it over if you go about it in a roundabout way. This way is more fun as it involves a bit of hacking knowledge and a bit of creative expertise to coax the information out in an effective manner that is full of smarts and swagger. Such methods are rarely employed when an individual is being targeted as common measures like phishing are effective enough but when the target in question is a large scale organization which has all the security measures in place that even the best efforts of the most experienced hackers. This will require a ground game with a radical paradigm shift. You can use many of the below mentioned techniques

Chatty Technicians:

This is the manner which is most used but requires a lot of confidence on part of the hacker. Not only will you have to take care of some heavy level logistics in the form of setting up an internet Skype number and a customer service type tone in greeting and gently guiding the client victim to hand over all his information that is important to you..

Social Spying:

Social spying is the name of that procedure which utilizes the pre conceived notions of the intended user to create leverage for your personal gain in order to acquire data. This technique is best employed against individuals as even small scale operations are well equipped to handle with all such attempts that use social spying. This because the IT department keeps tabs on all such advances and is less gullible to be deceived by any such maneuvers.

Garbage Collecting:

We have mentioned throughout the text that there are many soft wares and programs by which data on the hard disk can be wiped off such as Eraser along with stressing the need to have your hard drive formatted from time to time. But most people would not have read this e-book or are not that smart. You can exploit that to your advantage as the hard disks and other storage devices are a bounty for hackers as the information on them remains for a long time even if the entire recycle bin is deleted. Just running the recovery program from a remote computer or spy mode with you being physically present to retrieve the information. Sniffing: A sniffer is a system and/or gadget that screen all data passing through a computer system. It sniffs the information passing through the system off the wire and figures out where the information is going. Sniffers may have additional elements that empower them to channel a certain sort of information or catch passwords. A few sniffers (for instance, the FBI's disputable mass-observing apparatus Carnivore) can even modify records sent over a system, for example, an email or Web page.

How Does a Sniffer Work?

A sniffer is a software and/or program whose function is to complete a screening of all information that passes through a standalone computer or a system framework. It detects the data which passes through the system and determines

Computer Hacking

the flow of information. Sniffers have additional powers incorporated within them which act to channel certain types of code/data and catch passwords for which the algorithm has been previously set. The sniffers used by hackers are small time with the large sniffer programs being powered by a mainframe computer server that has the ability to alter the correspondence committed over an enclosed or open system. An example of such a large sniffer would be 'Carnivore' that is currently used by FBI.

For a sniffer to work effectively on any system it is important for the said system to have a system card that runs on a unique mode, also known as wanton mode, meaning it has the ability to get all the activity transferred over the system. A typical system card will just be aware of all the information that is or has been sent to the specific system address. This system address is properly known as the Media Access Control (MAC) address. You can does this on your own by just going to the particular MAC by going to the Windows Taskbar and clicking Start>Run> then, writing winipcfg (for Windows 95/98/ME) or ipconfig/all (for Windows NT/2000/.NET Server). The term physical location is also used for the MAC location

Another method is to think of a sniffer as a bipolar personality located in a particular advanced psych ward. One personality is the individual who will lend you an ear and hear what you are saying and respond in kind when he is respectfully included in the ongoing conversation. This individual is compared with a system card which runs on an unbridled mode. Moreover, if this individual is particularly interested in listening for a specific matter within that conversation then he will always pick up the matter that he is really interested in; similar to a sniffer in our analogy as it will always catches the data related to passwords

Types of Viruses Can Be Used in Hacking

What is a Computer Virus?

The computer virus is amongst the most well-known malware becoming part of the common slang. As such people tend to label all such malware that may have infected their computer as a virus which may not be always the case. The virus is indeed the most common malware to affect any individual computer or a computer network. Such is its presence that all computer protective software is termed as anti-virus. So what is a virus? A virus is any line of code which has been installed on the system or framework without the consent of the user and has the purpose of causing the malfunctioning of the system. The virus, like its biological counterpart, has the ability to replicate itself and transfer itself via the intranet, the internet, or simply via USB. What distinguishes a virus from any nonsense code is the fact that a virus was made by a human with the intent of causing harm rather than not functioning at all. Without such a versatility in its destructive ability, it may seem amazing to know that a virus is really simple to create but do not be fooled by its simplicity: Virus can be extremely lethal since they tend to take up all the available ROM and put the network or the computer to a stop as far as operation is concerned. There are different types of viruses but can be broadly divided into simple and complex viruses as for hacking purposes. Simple viruses tend to affect only one computer and are not having the ability to replicate. These are easily spotted by anti-virus program and the best suite for this purpose is by Norton. The other type of virus, Complex viruses, are having the ability to replicate and can transfer from one computer to another over various networks.

Infection - Infection - A program to software that when present within a computer or system can replicate itself to infect different directories. Unlike a virus which can transmit through a USB or over the Internet if downloaded by another computer, infections tend to retain themselves to a system when introduced. Therefore, it is wrong to group every error that comes in your computer as an infection as that is a layman terminology and it is strongly advised to use the correct term when describing the ailment such as virus, Trojan, malware etc.

Sorts of Viruses:-

The different sorts of infections are as per the following

1) Boot Sector Virus: - Boot sector viruses are meant to target the master boot record of the storage unit of the computer which can be the hard drive or mass storage unit. The boot record code that is responsible for maintaining the function of the system framework is overrun by the boot sector virus. The way this virus causes the above mentioned action is either by copying the viral code of the boot sector virus onto the master boot program code or by copying the very same viral code onto a specific piece of hard drive adjacent to the main functional unit of the hard drive controlled by the boot sector program and overwriting it with the viral code. They consequence of such an action by the virus is that the computer will fail to boot when started or a less dire result will be that the computer has a distorted result of the graphical user interface rendering it effectively useless. Examples of boot- division viruses are Michelangelo and Stoned.

2) File or Program Viruses: - Not all viruses cause the fatal action of boot sector viruses and the rest usually fill niches that perform an action that fill a specific niche that cause harm to a file, program or document. These viruses inflict these program or files which when opened or executed cause the virus to be activated in the memory and perform whatever action that has been written un their underlying code to damage the system framework. The potential targets of these viruses include files having extensions such as .exe, .com, .bin, .drv, and .sys. Some prominent file and program viruses are Sunday and Cascade.

3) Multipartite Viruses: - A multipartite virus, as the name suggests is a computer infection that targets the functionality of the system in various steps of its specific action concerning a singular or multifaceted execution, and thus is forming a roadblock on the entire coded path rendering the whole process completely corrupt. Therefore, it is easily understood that this virus is affecting both parts of the program, the hidden code which processes its output and also the output itself by doubling on the harm. This understanding of the concept is vital for developers as only then does this virus become all-encompassing in its action and necessitates the anti-virus program to destroy all portions of the inflicted parts of the program as attacked by the multipartite virus, without which the effect of the program will still remain.

Different examples of the multipartite virus are Invader, Flip.

4) Stealth Viruses: - These viruses are like the experienced hacker; they employ different techniques in getting the job done and are not unilateral in their approach. Moreover, they use different techniques in hiding themselves from anti-virus programs utilizing varying forms to avoid detection. Many free antiviruses available are unable to detect this virus as it easily switches between normal programming modes where it is not suspected during the virus scan to the lethal version where it can cause its damage.

5) Polymorphic Viruses: - - The night crawler of the viruses as it has the unique ability to transform itself and therefore prevent detection from any anti-virus program. The viral code underlying its functionality is mutated from time to time when remaining within a particular system and also when it is transmitted from one computer to another. It is one of the most persistent viruses due to this property of transformation and can remain within part of a framework network for a long time.

6) Macro Viruses: - As the macro suggests, the target of the virus is on a big scale. Macro viruses tend to infect a large computer software or program such as Microsoft Office, Adobe Reader etc. This macro virus causes to set in motion a cascade of activity that is put in motion when the targeted program is opened or activated. Though this virus may seem far reaching in its targeted results but they are mostly harmless as only a slight decrease in functionality is the outcome which is tolerated by the end user as a glitch in the program code prompting him to either update, which is useless as the macro virus remains within the application, or to delete and reinstall. Examples include Concept Virus and Melissa Worm

Chapter 5: Tips for Ethical Hacking

You need to have a sense of principled justice in your hacking to succeed whether that is against the framework of an employer or doing it for practice in improving your skill. If you ingrain the below mentioned points in your profession, then not only will you have peace of mind but also no added worries of being persecuted as the careless beginner hacker leaves around clues that can be used to incriminate you :

- Have informed consent before carrying out a hack against a client's system or even your friend's computer. This is a point most looked over even by the most experienced hacker but should be the first thing on your mind. Get the permission to carry out your trade in clear explicit terms, most favorably in the form of a hard copy. If paper is not the modus operandi then a thorough explanation of the things you are about to do and the possible risks involved in any hack should be made very clear to the person asking for your expertise. This may seem a useless exercise, especially if doing it for someone you know but be warned, any evidence that you leave behind can and probably will be used against you in a court of law. The judiciary has an updated code of conduct in what to do with cases pertaining to digital crime and you certainly do not want to end up on the wrong side of the law. I cannot stress this point enough that your life is most important to protect and anyone who has seen Die Hard 4 will certainly get my this understanding. People have been known to get the services of newbie hackers and bring up a case against them to get damages or to put the gullible hacker behind bars, for fun. It is a terrible world out there so it is best to get some information on how to protect yourself from getting sued for your services. First, consult a lawyer who handles cases like these as practical knowledge of knowing the kind of trouble hackers get into is a good start. Secondly, search on the internet for a hacking consent form which you can tailor for your business and get it signed before doing anything else.

- Having put up a backup plan if your client turns the table on you, the next step is to ensure that the job you are going to do is to the best of your ability. The last thing you want is to slack off and procrastinate while your client constantly peppers you with queries as to how the work is coming along. This is accomplished by setting up milestones and check posts to chart your progress so that you can update the client with the appropriate information instead of

Computer Hacking

coming up with excuses. Along with that, it never hurts to clarify the time it will take and set the client's expectations at a reasonable level as you do not have a magic wand to wave away all problems pertaining to security infrastructure of the network or individual framework. As the slogan goes, under promise and over deliver.

- It takes more than a computer and wicked typing skills to hack. This is something that has been made clear throughout the text but is unfortunately forgotten when the hacker gets about doing it, especially for work. If you are going to break through a firewall or boost up the security loopholes, always research rather than relying on sheer memory. Hacking manuals are available that succinctly describe the steps in which certain commonplace tasks are to be performed. Always have the necessary programs and software installed before beginning and make sure to have the latest updates installed. It won't do you harm if you make the effort to be prepared in your approach.

- If you are going to provide your service to a company in safeguarding their network against cyber-attacks, it is best to advise them that the testing of your installed defenses is best carried out when the stock market is in the black or when the sales are doing well. Because as you may well know, it is only in success that envious eyes are turned towards you and that is when your client is at most risk of being at the receiving end of a hacking assault. So you may very well do the job on any given Sunday but be sure to remind them to call you when the going is good. Only then will your task be truly complete.

- If you want to be secure, think like the enemy. As you progress through your training and follow up certain discussions on Internet forums, you will get to know of the ways and methods by which the infamous and notorious hackers carry out the most destructive havoc imaginable. Suffice to say, these hackers have attained demi god status and their acts are case studies on how to come up with ingenious methods of wreaking computer security protocols apart. As you shore up the security of your client's network, always keep in mind the dangers that lurk in the shadows. It is only by being aware of the enemy's arsenal can you think of any loopholes that are almost always there. It is a given that despite your best efforts, there will be an attack that you could not have prevented. You can bear that. But what is intolerable and will cause your reputation much harm is your slip up against current threats. So be sure to brush up on the latest threats doing the rounds. Only by following this guideline can you give the surety that a framework has been adequately secured.

- Though mentioned in the previous point, it is worth mentioning on its own as hackers tend to get a lot of slack because of it. You are the best at what you do but such is the nature of technology that a new danger will always spring up. Like global health pandemics, the technology world is not immune from such an event. So be sure to make it clear that no security is foolproof. You have to regularly update it. Kind of like a vaccine shot!

- Once you have put up the security parameters and tightened all present loopholes, it comes down to testing your work. Many hackers take it upon themselves to do the testing without getting the client involved. Huge Mistake! Always keep the people involved in the know as they assume that the hacker is to be blamed for any lapses that will occur thereafter. Explain fully and without hacking jargon the steps you have done to test your measures. This will prevent you from suffering any headaches.

- The computer can be secured to the brim with all sorts of software and programs but that all will come to not if the users of the system do not take common sense measures. Most of the mistakes will pertain to not using the computer in the way it should be used. Using common place passwords, like 'Password 'or 'ABC123' would be hacked in a matter of seconds. Make you to educate the users about these issues so that the system would not become a sitting duck. Another common mistake, which us hackers assume to be a given, is to not turn off the computer once you are leaving for work. Be sure to point this one out as you will be surprised to know how many people are so careless.

- In the process of working of securing the client's system framework, you will be exposed to data of all employees. It is your responsibility to not misuse your immense power for your own personal gain when you have been trusted with such a delicate situation. Moreover, you have to extremely careful to not let your guard down that people can exploit your position to access that information.

- Up till now we have focused on the necessary precautions you have to take in order to be the best at your job. But what about the task at hand? Never be so mundane in your approach and have flexibility in solving the problem. Many times you will encounter obstacles that seemingly cannot be solved. Do not despair and take a deep breath. Go back to the basics and break it down into small parts and tackle them step by step.

- Once you find the loopholes it is your utmost imperative to report them immediately to the company officials or the person in charge before fixing them. You will not get credit for troubles you solved by yourself without bringing into attention. First make the problem apparent and once the same has been recognized by your client, then you can get about putting in place the necessary safety measures.

- With all things said and done, there are undeniable skills that have no relation to hacking but are something you have to be good at in order to succeed. Show your employers that you are extremely grateful for the opportunity to work with them and will welcome any other assignment they may have in the future. Make them aware of the precautions they have to take against hacking and the latest harms that can infect their networks.

Hacking is a great way to make money as there are many business opportunities that you can use for your advantage. Conform to any laws that may apply to you and be sure to do great work. Your reputation will grow exponentially; you will be raking in bucket loads of cash and have a great time doing the thing you love so dearly.

Chapter 6: Hacking Self Defense

You can be the strongest fighter in all the lands but you are only as strong as your weakest link. Achilles found out the hard way. So be sure to save your heel from any arrow attacks. Many infections are known to enter the system framework by very complex ways against which the diligent hacker may come up with adequate defenses but what about people whose only concern are to send an occasional email and work on tables in Excel? The documents we transfer from USB and receive from email are the most common innocent methods of infecting the computer. The hacker or the computer enthusiast will surely take precautionary measures but the common user who is not at all concerned with issues pertaining to computer security. So at the end of this book, before proceeding further, if there is one thing you should learn that common sense prevails over everything else and always take the simple precautions. Never be lazy in covering all your bases and check to make sure that any downtime or infection that tend to occur from time to time are not caused by a lapse of attention to minor detail.

Having set the tone for an intimate discussion on the measures to take in protecting yourself digitally, we have to start off with the most aspect of data. It is truly the age of data where everyone is consuming it in amounts unimaginable a few decades ago. Everything is at the push of a button, nay, at your touch with touchscreens. Taking photos, videos along with important documents and files running into terabytes, it was inevitable that sooner or later our approach towards safeguarding them would become callous. It is therefore imperative on us not to download shady software and programs and always keep passwords on all of them to prevent accidental access.

Talking of keeping data under locks becomes all the more difficult seeing that the social media age has well and truly arrived. While previously there was only MySpace, Facebook and Twitter, the number of social networking sites has spiraled out of control with Snapchat, LinkedIn, LineChat, Whatsapp, Hike etc. With great power to create revolutions like the Arab Spring, there also comes great responsibility to protect you. Never ever mention the names of your dearest and closest on these above mentioned and any other such sites. Not only can those willing to exploit you will use these names to search them and come up with data to blackmail you but they will put these names in password breaking algorithms to access your account on these social websites and damage your repute. The same vigilance applies to your bio data like your DOB, place of birth, profession, the school or college you want to, the name of your pet dog, your favorite actor... the list really goes on and on as such information can more than easily be used to correctly answer the security questions and therefore gain access to the accounts, social media or financial. It does not take a genius to figure out that whenever you forget your password, the pre-determined question that you set eons ago had an answer you could give in your sleep and is something that is well known about you. No need to plaster it all over the Internet in the form of status updates, blog posts etc.

Just react to those you know or can identify

The fact is that you cannot avoid being connected to the Internet but you can always avoid people who are out there to irritate you and possibly scam you in one way or the other. First thing is to ramp up the privacy setting in all of your social media accounts so that no one can unnecessarily like your profile pictures or comment on your every status. If somebody shows stalker tendencies, it is best to block that person permanently. Always set up multiple email accounts and assign a function to each one. One can be for signing up to newsletters, the other for official business meetings and another for family and friends. That way you can separate the nonsense from things that are really important and savings hours from having to navigate through junk mail to find your boss' business proposal. The only way to make this arrangement work is to remember which email account you have for top level stuff and the one which you can give to the creepy guy on the subway.

Change Your Passwords

I trust the reader of this e-book to be tech savvy enough to not be foolish enough in having his password set in stone for the last 3 years and that same password being used for all his accounts. And if you are the person that has his password set to 'password', then I have nothing but pity for you. Seriously, search for a good password manager online and it pays in the long run to cough up some dough for a subscription fees to be on the safe side. Be sure to change your password ever so often, like in every 3 weeks or so, in order to have a bullet proof wall against invasion of your digital privacy. Follow some general guidelines in setting up the passwords like being longer than 8 characters, the password being a mix of upper and lower case letters along with using number combinations.

Be mindful with network

Like any neighborhood which you are not familiar with, the internet can be a dark and dangerous place. As we shift all lives onto this ever expanding landscape of webpages, it is best to be mindful with your money. When shopping online on sites like Amazon, always make sure that the website is 'https' and is not a fake website. To minimize your losses, always shop with prepaid credit cards like Payoneer or gift cards so that the person who hacks your information does not have unlimited access to all the money in your account or to the credit limit.

And from time to time, make it a habit to shut down your network so that your computer or smartphones are off the grid for some time when they are not in use. Malware gets an easy target when the device is idle or on standby, not powered off, but still have the Wi-Fi on.

Secure Your Network

It is all well and good to secure your dealings on the Internet but it is also to make sure that the way you get on the Internet also has all the bells and whistles. Nearly every home is connected to the Internet in one way or the other. We use it for different purposes like interaction, working, and enjoyment. But the security we assign to these remote connection hubs is dismal to say the least. The fact is we spend more time physically securing our house than we do securing the Internet and Wi-Fi networks of our homes leaving it to be exploited by criminals. We cannot wish these elements but we can take safety measures to ensure that they internet networks of our home are given the best protection so that no one steal the Internet for which you have paid for or use it for scrupulous purposes leaving you to be implicated in a crime in which you had no part or role.

Starting with the obvious, always have a password on your wireless connections. Do not just go with the default password that comes from the manufacturer but be sure to set it to your liking as soon you have installed it. As noted in the previous chapter, Wi-Fi can be very easy to hack so it is imperative upon you to make sure that a lengthy password is set having a combination of upper and lower case letters along with numbers and other characters. The length should be long and the password stored on a .txt file which can be opened when you have to share it with a friend or guest. Now that we have the home base covered, the same common sense applies to using Wi-Fi in public places. Don't. These free Wi-Fi hotspots are breeding ground hackers to test out their newly created spyware so it is best to avoid using them unless it is absolutely necessary. Another precaution: always have your credit cards covered with an aluminum foil so as to not be intercepted by hackers prowling around with an antenna set ready to gather such information.

We mentioned the use of Eraser software to clear away your data stored on your hard drive in the preceding chapters but it is also worth your while to format the hard disk from time to time just to be on the safe side as you can never be too safe.

Hacking the Hackers

For readers in the US of A, it is pertinent to mention that hacking is a crime under federal law, Computer Fraud and Abuse Act with variations as to the implementation from state to state. Undeterred, Hackers continue to use their skills in the technology arena to outsmart even the most solid of defenses and thus setting in place a cat and mouse game of new and secure firewalls and protocols being made which are hacked and the cycle goes on and on. The reasons for partaking in such activities range from playing a prank on a friend to possibly getting away with millions of dollars. For those who have forgotten the story told earlier, the tale of a group of Bangladeshi hackers who planned to steal one billion dollars of Bengali money kept with the Us Federal Reserve Bank is just a drop in the ocean.. Hackers either go solo or congregate in groups, and are almost always self-trained. Hackers have been portrayed extensively in popular media starting from the cult classic War Games in 1983 to the recently released The Social Network in which a young Mark Zuckerberg hacks the Harvard group online to start his billion dollar company.